D1228636

DISCARD

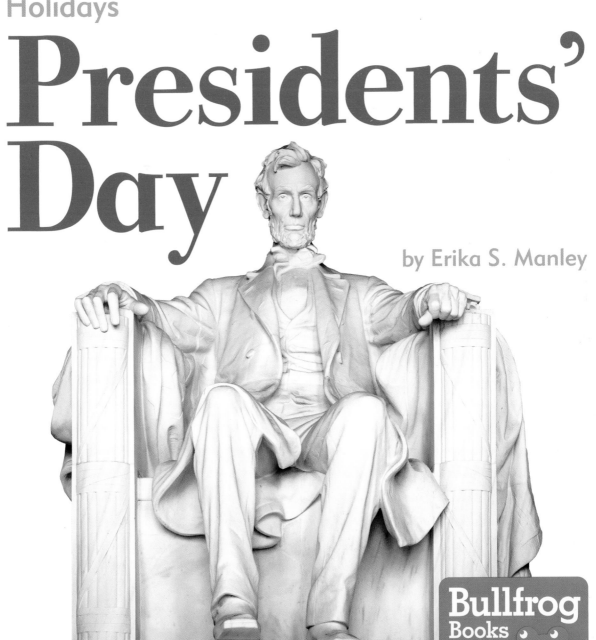

Holidays

Presidents' Day

by Erika S. Manley

Bullfrog Books

Ideas for Parents and Teachers

Bullfrog Books let children practice reading informational text at the earliest reading levels. Repetition, familiar words, and photo labels support early readers.

Before Reading

- Discuss the cover photo. What does it tell them?

- Look at the picture glossary together. Read and discuss the words.

Read the Book

- "Walk" through the book and look at the photos. Let the child ask questions. Point out the photo labels.

- Read the book to the child, or have him or her read independently.

After Reading

- Prompt the child to think more. Ask: Do you celebrate Presidents' Day? What do you do?

Bullfrog Books are published by Jump!
5357 Penn Avenue South
Minneapolis, MN 55419
www.jumplibrary.com

Copyright © 2018 Jump! International copyright reserved in all countries. No part of this book may be reproduced in any form without written permission from the publisher.

Library of Congress Cataloging-in-Publication Data

Names: Manley, Erika S., author.
Title: Presidents' Day / by Erika S. Manley.
Description: Bullfrog Books edition. | Minneapolis, MN: Jump!, Inc., [2018] | Series: Holidays | Includes index. | Audience: Grades K-3. | Audience: Ages 5-8. Identifiers: LCCN 2017027714 (print) LCCN 2017027864 (ebook) | ISBN 9781624966675 (ebook) | ISBN 9781620318362 (hbk.: alk. paper) ISBN 9781620318379 (pbk.)
Subjects: LCSH: Presidents' Day—Juvenile literature. | Classification: LCC E176.8 (ebook) LCC E176.8 .M16 2018 (print) | DDC 394.261—dc23
LC record available at https://lccn.loc.gov/2017027714

Editors: Jenna Trnka & Jenny Fretland VanVoorst
Book Designer: Leah Sanders
Photo Researcher: Leah Sanders

Photo Credits: dbimages/Alamy, cover (left); Elnur/Shutterstock, cover (right); S.Borisov/Shutterstock, 1; Arvind Balaraman/Shutterstock, 3; Paul B. Moore/Shutterstock, 4; nito/Shutterstock, 5; Marcio Jose Bastos Silva/Shutterstock, 6–7, 23bl; Jose Luis Pelaez Inc/Getty, 8–9 (foreground); Pammy Studio/Shutterstock, 8–9 (background); Wavebreakmedia/iStock, 10–11 (background); Volina/Shutterstock, 10–11 (foreground); NurPhoto/Getty, 12–13; Everett Collection Historical/Alamy, 14, 23tr; Nicole S Glass/Shutterstock, 15; LWA/Dann Tardif/Getty, 16–17; Dann Tardif/Getty, 18; Ryan McVay/iStock, 19, 23br; Sergey Novikov/Shutterstock, 20–21; GraphicaArtis/Getty, 22l; Everett - Art/Shutterstock, 22m, 23mr; ClassicStock/Alamy, 22r; CatLane/iStock, 24.

Printed in the United States of America at Corporate Graphics in North Mankato, Minnesota.

RO452564999

Table of Contents

What Is Presidents' Day?

Presidents' Day is a U.S. holiday.

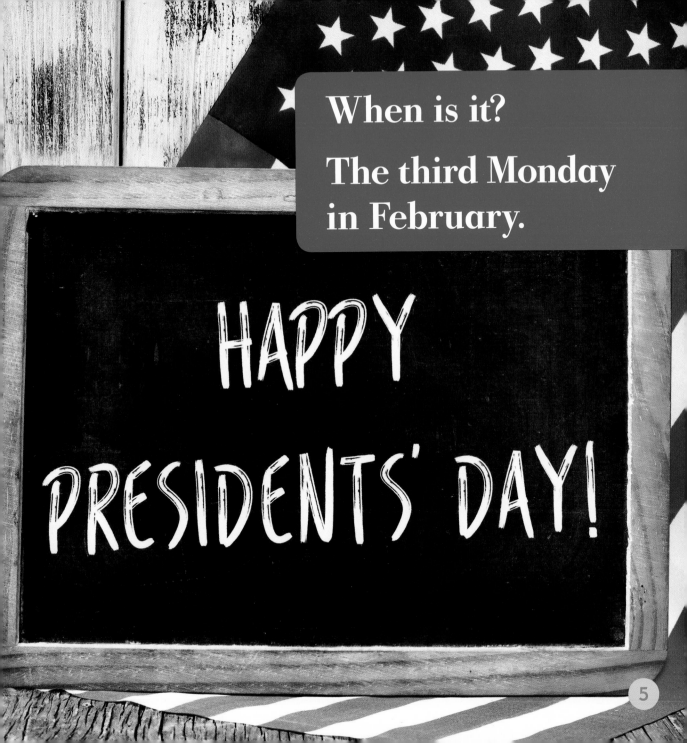

When is it?

The third Monday in February.

5

George
Washington

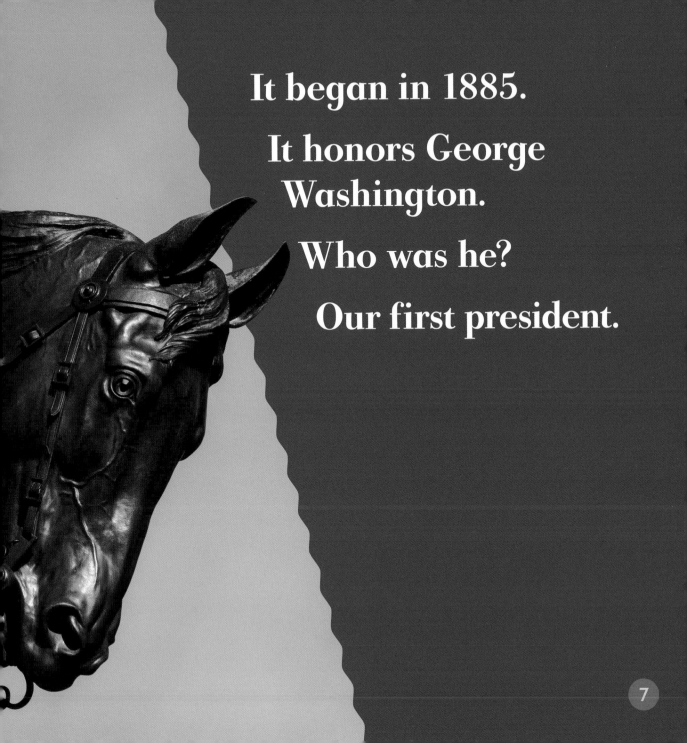

It began in 1885.

It honors George Washington.

Who was he?

Our first president.

Look!

His face is on the dollar.

Washington

A state is named for him.

Many cities are, too.

We call him the father
of our country.

Dwight D. Eisenhower

They sign laws.

14

Donald Trump

They meet with other leaders.

How do we celebrate?

Mae's class draws.

Ben acts in a play.

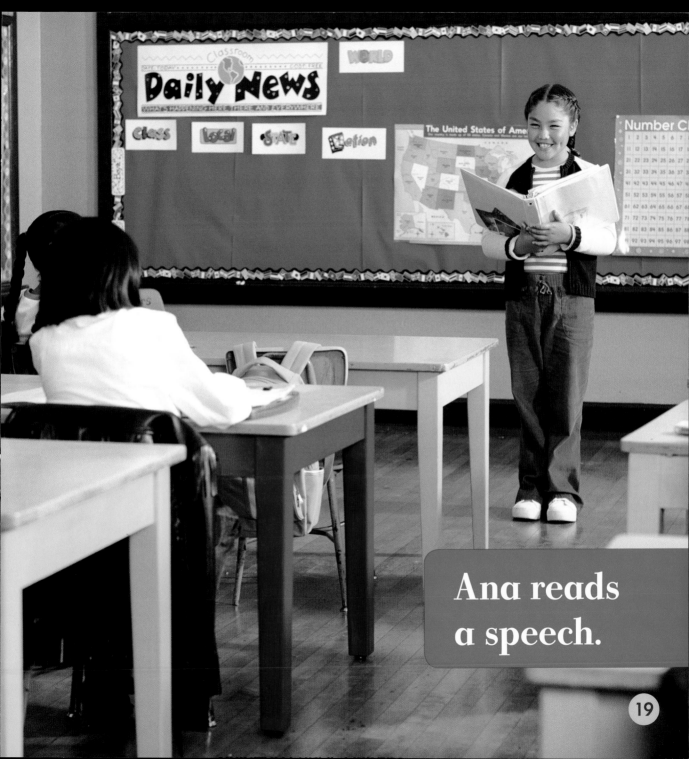

Ana reads
a speech.

It is a special day!

Our Presidents

The three presidents most closely tied to Presidents' Day are George Washington, Thomas Jefferson, and Abraham Lincoln.

Thomas Jefferson was president from 1801 to 1809. He wrote the Declaration of Independence. It said the United States was free from Great Britain.

Abraham Lincoln was president from 1861 to 1865. He signed the Emancipation Proclamation. It freed slaves in the United States.

George Washington was president from 1789 to 1797. He was the country's first president.

Picture Glossary

honors
Treats with respect.

president
The head of state of a country.

laws
Rules the government makes for communities to follow.

speech
A public talk.

Index

To Learn More

Learning more is as easy as 1, 2, 3.

1) Go to www.factsurfer.com

2) Enter "Presidents'Day" into the search box.

3) Click the "Surf" button to see a list of websites.

With factsurfer.com, finding more information is just a click away.